Begin I must

THE JOURNEY

RHONDA LISS

Written by Rhonda Liss

Design, Layout and Illustrations: Marea Saldarriaga

The symbols appearing between poems are reimagined from Adinkra, traditional symbols of the Asante people of Ghana. With gratitude, we honor their cultural heritage and wisdom. May their meanings continue to guide and inspire.

ISBN: 979-8-218-79431-6

Contents

Introduction

In 2019, I was a retired educator and professional opera and theater singer who spent a lot of my time doing what I loved most: singing and performing cabaret. I was also the caretaker of my husband of almost 30 years, who was suffering from dementia. In May of that year, stepping out of a taxi in Oberlin, Ohio where I was about to attend my 50th college reunion, my cell phone rang. "You have to come home. Reid is in a coma and they don't think he's going to make it."

A week later we took him off life support. I spent the next 6 months emptying out my incredibly cluttered but beautiful home of 28 years, selling it and moving to Sarasota. One night while performing my cabaret "Life, Love and What I've Learned Along the Way," I opened my mouth and nothing came out. Niente, nada, zero. In over 60 years of singing that had never happened to me. Through sheer will, I managed to finish the show. Two months later, I was diagnosed with Parkinson's. And two months after that the whole country was in shutdown because of the pandemic and I was facing it alone.

I was certainly not a stranger to loss. I had lost my mother at the age of 12 and five years later, my father. But I had always had my singing to fulfill me and bring me untold joy. Parkinson's had deprived me of that.

So, I started telling stories through poetry and realized the positive power they had on my life. I was in charge, as I had always been, but now the stakes were higher. And I wanted to do more than just survive. I wanted to thrive, so healing became a full-time job.

I am now acting, writing, and producing. I have up to this point been able to keep the effects of Parkinson's at bay. I enjoy life to the fullest. And I have no intentions of ever giving in to the all-pervasive negativity in our society that will engulf us if we don't fight back.

R. LISS
New York City, New York
August 2025

PART ONE

Facing the Darkness

Between Dreams and Sleep

I wander along this bed at night,
hovering above the sheets,
floating like a lost soul
in search of a home.

I taste the inexactitude of it all,
wondering where I might alight
if I could see the ground.
No search lights to lead the way,
guiding me to a safe landing.

What is this place
between light and dark,
dreams and sleep?
One wrong turn,
Heart skips a beat,
A gasp of breath.

Where does this journey lead?
How far must I go to know
what is the truth of it all?

I recall a simpler time,
when sleep would caress me
and hold me
gently in her arms.
One, two, three,
and darkness would fall.

I would crawl like a snake,
piercing the deepest earth,
and feel the pull of roots
into paradise, my rebirth.
And wake as a newborn child,
with so much time ahead,
there was no dread
of what the future might bring.

Perhaps I'll grow wings.

The Waters of Babylon

The Waters of Babylon have not receded
and we continue to weep
and fight to keep ourselves afloat,
oar in hand,
trying to stay the course.
Our homeland,
as we knew it is gone,
no longer whole or strong
with love threading our souls together.
But a caldron of hatred and fear,
lashing out against the innocent,
never shedding a tear of compassion.

Is there no one to lead us to the other side?
Must we abide with tyrants
so cruelly wrong,
they will veil every truth,
tell any lie that will
keep them strong, in control,
at the helm,
steering us
into oblivion.

It is no surprise
that we are left
to sail down
this dark river of injustice.

The thin overalls
of hope and dread,
our new companions,
are now wed,
while we brace ourselves
against the storm,
trying to shed the skin
hardened by our sorrow,
trying to survive.

We yearn for the day
when we can step out of this boat
and slowly walk
on the dry, scorched land.
when the warmth of freedom
gives its hand
to melt the barriers between us,
when we can finally reach out
and touch the enemy.

Ode to Injustice: Tightening the Jar

Here is the jar.
Into it we put the rules,
the tools we will need to define a people, a group:
the blacks,
the old,
the immigrants,
the women,
the expendables.
And we turn the lid.

It started so far back.
Slaves from Africa,
strong, docile,
will work for nothing;
will pick our cotton,
cut our sugarcane.
They are not the same as us.
And so, greed won out
and we did not shout
but turned the lid a little tighter.

Now into this mix we put
auntie, boy.
No Miss, Mrs. or Madame.
There will be no respect.
What do they expect
when they are our toys.

A train wreck yesterday:
two men, two women were killed
and four Negroes.
Another twist.
Another Emmett Till.

And the men had whips.
They would not let go.
And the merchandise was sold on blocks
and the nameless were put in chains.
Erased was their humanity
and their families were torn apart.
Where was the heart?
How much torture can we fit into this jar?

And a great war was fought
to keep them down.
And the good men won,
and the vote was given.
And a small crack appeared.
But the die was cast.
These whites were scared,
and a piece of tape quickly covered
any taste of freedom.

The back of the bus,
the front of the train.
The rules kept on changing.
This is insane.
Then a bridge was crossed,

more protests, more marches
in the name of justice.
Now new cracks appeared
but the tape was used up
so, the evils dug deeper.
They disappeared
but had not given up.

By now the jar was overflowing
with children in cages,
with poverty and suffering growing.
Then the enemy reared its evil head
and found a new leader who would fight instead
to keep America white,
or at least surround the jar with a wall.
That was all he could do.

And new protesters took to the streets.
More whites than ever
joined to fight back
and the jar was completely broken.
They would never give up after the attacks
on law and democracy.
But the country was suffering,
millions infected, thousands dead
and cages still locked
and black lives shred
by the knives of injustice.

No, the jar cannot be repaired
and must not be
of that I am sure.
But what is the answer
what is the cure
for these centuries of misdeed?

We must not keep silent.
We must not follow.
We must instead lead.

The Streets of Boston

I walked these streets of Boston
so many years ago,
excited by the lure
of music and art
and wanted desperately
to know their mysteries
to make a start of my own.

As I entered the hall,
I could recall
the smell of gardenias
intoxicating the night.
And the purple haired ladies
who warmed me
with the sight of their smiles.

The conductor would raise his baton
and I was gone,
lost in a beauty
whose secret gardens
were just taking seed,
suckling on a breakfast
of Mozart and Brahms,
their colors not yet a part
of the palette I would need
to create my own gardens.

I was 12 and my roots
had been torn apart,
leaving only my music
to hold me in its arms
and lull me to sleep.

Autumn Leaves
the last song I had sung,
her favorite,
floated still
in the stifling room
already becoming a ghostly white.
It had soothed her failing heart
for a moment,
but it had not been enough
to stay her flight.

Yet she is here with me again
and will always be
As I walk
the streets of Boston.

Parting

Any way you slice it,
parting is not a piece of cake
or a hiccup at the end
of a grand
bottle of champagne
with a dizziness
that can drive you insane.
Rather it's a slow burning ache
flamed by the laughter
and loving we shared.

Anyway -
No pill you can take
will make it go away.
It doesn't seem to be
on any schedule
that I can detect
or bother about sleep cycles.
It doesn't even respect
my peace of mind.

Anyway -
I am on this journey
that digs deep into the past,
the shards left not easy to find,
the truth even harder to unmask.
Every day there is a new surprise,

a revelation,
a nightmare.
I can't even decide
where to begin.

Anyway -
Begin I must!
And I will have to trust
where this journey will lead
and follow my gut,
which has always been my guide.

Anyway -
Whatever "they" may say,
Parting is not a piece of cake.

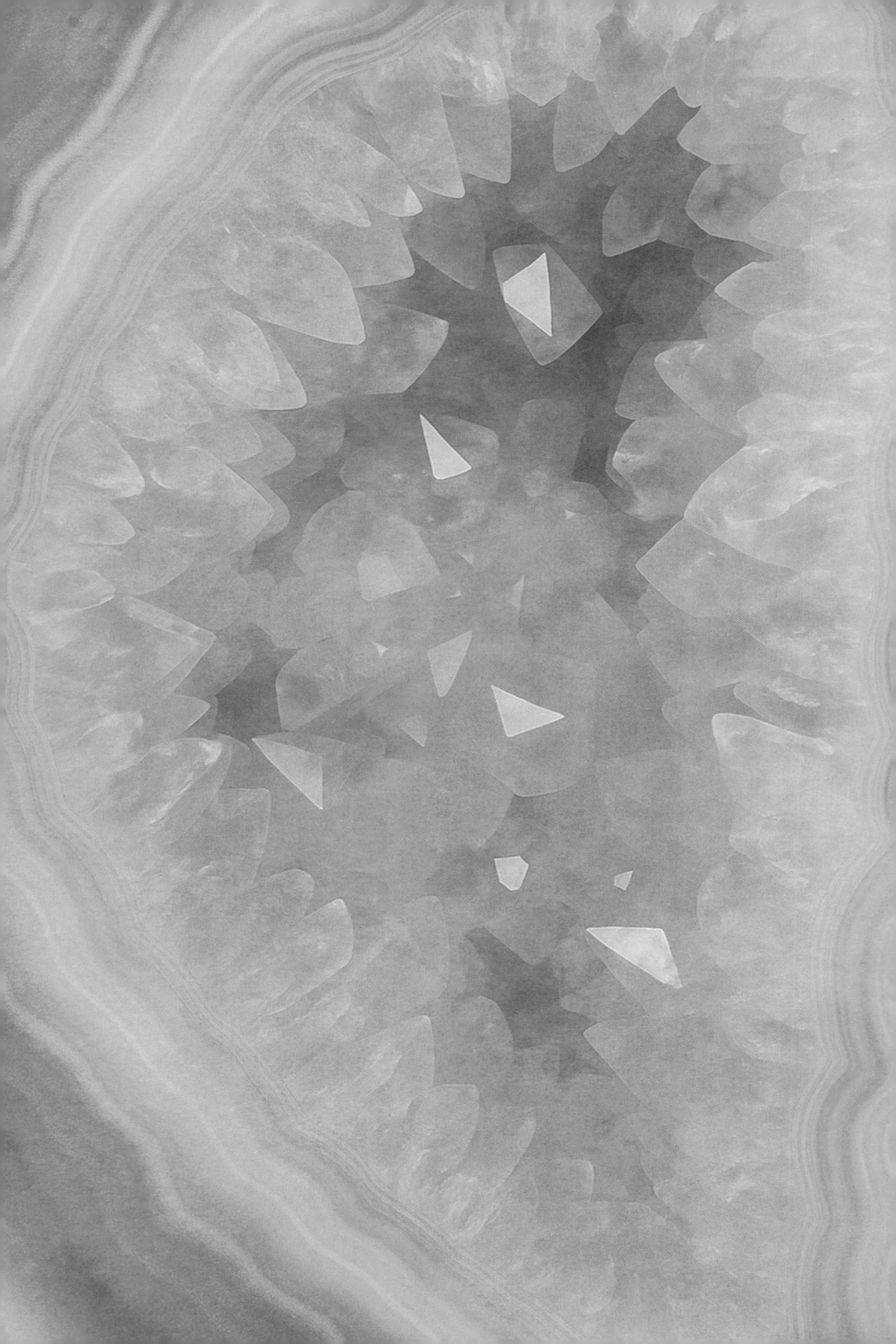

PART TWO

Reckoning and Transforming

The Older Woman

They say in France
that the older woman is valued,
takes pride in every line,
in every wrinkle.

Perhaps that was so once upon a time,
very long ago.

But think of Jeanne Moreau
in Jules and Jim
and how we watched every year,
gasping with fear,
as the sides of her mouth began to droop,
like the petals of a fragrant rose
pressed inside the pages of an old scrapbook,
its essence cradled in memories,
forever young and beautiful.

And then, of course, there was Catherine Deneuve,
who put on some pounds, lifted the face,
but somehow still exuded a grace,
a trace of her own type of sexuality,
as confident as an older woman can be
who's been placed on a postage stamp.

We are so bold as young women,
strutting proudly down the streets,
cats in heat,

secure in our immortality,
flush with the scent of wrinkled sheets,
basking in the power of our sex,
knowing how far we had come.

I remember the day, centuries
or was it minutes
after that dawn,
after the heat and cold of love and loss
had mapped out a different face,
scarred with battles waged,
with victories and defeats,
with hopes and fears
of where that street might end.

I have accepted the invitation
to walk down that street,
through the dusk, into the darkness
of an uncharted night,
not strutting,
but walking with the measured steps
of a dignity well-earned.

And I can sit down at the table with friends
who are sharing the same road,
and dine on our scrapbooks together.

The Virtue of The Stoics

I sit and stare at the trees
whose roots have commingled
over centuries of history,
and ponder the mystery that was,
is, and, will be me.
How can I find a clearing
in this tangled density?

The Stoics had it right,
Zeno and his lot,
as they proclaimed the four virtues.
You need courage and wisdom to stay at home
in this battle for sanity.
Courage not to open the door and explore
what tragedy might lie outside.
Not to look ahead in dread of
where this all will end.
You need temperance
not to sound the alarm,
but to stay calm
as you make you way
through the sometimes-endless hours
of a never-ending day.

What is the meaning of life?
What is in my power to create or erase?
How can I deal with my emotions
in the face of this adversity?

And so, I reflect on the past
and let it shine into this dark space:
the voice of my mother as she lit the Shabbat candles,
the flame making her pale face glow with red,
like the tomatoes my father lovingly planted in his garden

I smell the briny sea air
as I remember the night, I dare sneak out
to sleep on the shore -alone but not afraid.

And as I gaze up at the stars this night,
I am lulled by their voices
as the past comes in with the tide.
And I am comforted.

Don't Be Impatient with Genius

Better not be impatient with genius while it's growing,
cause you will miss the sowing pains
and the pieces of diamond
that are just heating up.

Better not be
so critical of the colt,
cause it's gonna bolt
out of the paddock
and give you a jolt
when you're not there to share its success
or hear the best damn
moment of beauty
that soars into the blue
leaving you alone
to stew on the plain.

Don't give us your sass,
cause they're gonna kick ass
and you'll be on the wrong page.

I know 's hard to play the sage
and be smart and gauge
where this is going.
But you ought to know.
Or so you told me many years ago.

Don't be so hard on imperfection
because on further inspection
the filet is still raw.
It needs to thaw
in its own time.
You see.
Every ingredient is there.
You need to be fair
and wait for the chef
to go through the stages
of adding the spice
and letting it simmer
till it's nice and tasty.
So, don't be hasty.

For where were you at twenty-five?
Certainly not the finished product
in all its crowning glory.
You were at the beginning of your story.
And so are they.

So, don't be so impatient with genius.

Unexpected

Life seems to be full of these crazy twists and turns.
It's a roller coaster ride
where you just might slide
into an unknown whirlpool,
trying to pull you down
or maybe throw you up in the air,
where there's no one to catch you
and you might not even be spared
a breath of calm air.
Ah give me an OM.

Will I crash into the sea
and tangle with the fish,
dishing up some fresh fantasy
of whaling tales from long ago?

I don't know,
but I seem to get pulled around,
shaken not stirred
into a cocktail
of dubious worth.
What a dearth of clarity.
Someone calls and says one thing
when they really mean something else.
Will there ever be a neat little row of answers
that arrive on time and I can put on a shelf?

But the shelf would soon become a pile,
of more tragic tales.
That is the style
that this chaos of adventures will take.

So, I must stay awake the best I can,
and sort through this mischief
of games and claims on my sanity.

And learn to create my own reality
I can rely upon.
Not lost in the stars
or stranded on Mars,
but one with a clearer chart,
to help me thrive and make a fresh start.

Partaking

What I like about partaking
is that the part you've become
is ready to share.
Whether it's here or there.
And for the sweetness to stay
There needs to be more play
But not only far away.

One fact is that
we both swim in the sea
and need to be free
to continue our creativity

Yet in the middle of the night
when my arm reaches out
in the darkness
there is no one
to hold me tight
and make the world
feel all right.

You asked me one day
if we would always
laugh this way,
If this magic moment would stay.
I said that there is only one beginning,
only one first time

when something is new,
the round shiny toy,
ready to give joy
at a moment's notice.

But it's only the first inning
of a game that could go on
and become strong
if we wanted it to.

Here's what I know.
I am always changing.
That part is true.
I am who I have become.
That part is new.

But I am also
who I have always been
and will always be:
Deeply emotional.
That is me.

PART THREE

Emergence and Renewal

Yellow

At first, I could not admit to loving yellow.
There is not one article of clothing in my closet
that attacks with that blaring color.

Or for that matter any other
towel or sheet or plate.
Perhaps I saw it as too present,
too noisy to contemplate,
and feared its dazzle might
actually, outshine mine
so, I preferred not to take the chance.

Yet I will admit a certain softness
as I glance
at the yellow daffodils,
spreading sunshine over that mountain trail
one early spring
of my youth.
Or the yellow of the first canary
I had, who refused to sing
and then died,
quite suddenly in its cage
one bleak winter morning.

And the leaves of the quaking aspen in fall,
equaled only by the autumn gold ginkgo tree,
and even the American Elm anointed me
entering the realm of life's last glow
before it all drifted away.

And surely, I must ponder on
the sunlight shining
through the window of my room.
Does it really come from that fiery yellow orb?
And the Yellow rose of Texas
which was brought from China,
another factoid that is hard to absorb.

Yet now as I even try to complain,
there is no memory more magical
that equals the golden rain,
a tree so gracefully ringing,
like coins falling through the sky
playing on the breeze a song of longing.
Or an ever-haunting lullaby.

Sacred Space

I don't need an organ
playing under a vaulted roof.
Nor windows stretching up to the sky
or prisms of light carried on sunbeams.

But let a special melody pierce me
with a love and pain and beauty so pure
that I feel my heart pried open
like an oyster shell
letting in the pearls of peace and belonging
that connect me to the earth,
and all those lonely wanderers
looking for a place
where they can take off their shoes
and rest their feet.

I sat on a hillside a while ago
next to a friend of over 50 years.
We opened some wine
as we popped salty peanuts into our mouths
after a day of sharing stories and art.
Then told a few more,
unmasking some hidden memories of our past,
wondering how two people so different
could share a poem by Byron.

And there we sat side by side,
silently watching the sun go down.

I walked through the woods close to the shore,
watched an osprey bring food to its young.
My eye caught a squirrel scurrying up a tree,
the yellow and orange leaves
glowing in the sun.
And all I could hear
were the sounds of the waves
and the beating of my heart.

The New World to Be

The Buddhists say our minds are full of noise,
a cacophony of dos and don'ts,
of desires and hate,
that we need to meditate and go inside.
But how can I hide
from this raging sea

Where every blade of grass
cuts like a scythe
through a morass of ignorance and lies.
There is much to despise.
What should we save?
What should we erase?
What will take its place
in a New World that could be?

Can we erase the images of
children trying to find clean water in a camp
where there are no buckets and no soap?
Or an angry mob with its AK-47 rifles,
willing to shoot through
the hearts of humanity and reason?
The human casualties of disease and war.

Let us even the score
with those driven by greed and fear
of equality and justice so great

they would not hesitate to cut down every tree,
or anyone who does not agree
with their distorted take on reality.

Let us save those who would risk their lives for all.
Not just white, not just black,
who will always have your back,
who will bend to pick up the smallest seed
to nourish a society starved for a taste of sky.
Who will cherish the earth and understand why,
as they move forward toward the healing of this universe,
toward harmony and peace.

Museum of Happiness

A songbird stunned me on this rainy morning,
and I, still stiff from a fitful sleep,
the infant day just dawning,
was about to make my daily list
of oughts and shoulds and coulds and cants,
all the things I had to do,
and other proletarian rants.

But I was ready, and the song was sweet,
a warming pull at my two cold feet.
"There is a place you need to go," it said,
and a ray of sunshine made me smile
as I jumped so gaily out of bed.

A new museum has opened its doors,
a place of do-what-you-want,
a place where imagination soars.

The museum of happiness is here,
filled with risks you're allowed to take,
with paths that lead to magic lanes,
and surprise encounters on enchanted planes.

So make a wish, look inside your panoply of dreams,
and you may find what you're searching for
amidst more devious schemes.

An Octopus's Garden

It has been handed down in our ancient lore
that a song was written about a garden of yore,
under the sea in the shade.

Well, since you're so curious today,
you may certainly stay
with me here by the shore,
and I'll tell you even more
of my fascinating tale.

My eyes wide open are almost human,
very similar to yours, an example of evolution,
although from widely different starting points.
Now don't get yourself out of joint.
We are not in competition.

In fact, I have 8 arms and neurons galore,
more than any other invertebrates,
500 million will almost even the score
with some monkeys whom you have always vetted
as the closest to man and worthy to be petted.

Well, I am inquisitive and friendly,
much like dolphins or dogs,
and yes, I'm a mollusk,
so never confuse me with frogs.

I am notoriously feisty,
learning many new skills,
like pulling a clam apart to get at my food.
I can do that at will!

And as for color, I am not just black or white.
I can change to blue, to pink or red,
and I am intelligent,
but different from you,
so get that fact into your silly little head.

Some say we look alien,
but we can change our skin and our texture,
and my suckers can grasp and taste.
Okay, I'm giving you a lecture.

Nothing in my skeleton goes to waste,
because I have no bones except, of course,
those protecting my prodigious brain.
And I can vanish in a flash,
which drives my predators insane.
In fact, my amazing ability to disappear
once got me stuck in a can of beer.

As a female, of which I am very proud,
I will lay a clutch of 200 eggs,
and then holler out loud:
"This is my beginning and my end."
Then for over four years I will defend
my babes as they grow strong and survive.

And I will wither and die
just to keep them alive.

I have lived these five years
and enjoyed the adventure
without anxiety or worry,
unlike yours, I would venture to say.
No religion, no politics, no racist fights.
So, are you just a little bit jealous?
Oh yes, and no sleepless nights!

Alone but Not Lonely

I am alone today but not lonely.
Perhaps that will start,
but I will keep myself 6 feet apart
and share the thoughts
that dwell inside
with the friends that are near and far
and realize how important they are to keeping me alive.

I heard a story yesterday about introversion
and all the joys that could bring.
A house full of books with time to contemplate
to create and relate the stories that go back in time.

Today too many of us communicate in bites.
Have we lost the taste for the whole meal
Afraid it might steal another second
from the superficial surface we slide upon.
Afraid to share face to face.

How ironic that we are now in this place
where holding hands cannot be,
where we are floating in a sea
of unpredictability
knowing not which shore
we will land upon
or even if it will be gone before we descend.

I will continue to explore the depths of the sea inside.
And because I have been given the gift of time
allow the seeds to grow
into moments of wonder at what I now can see,
a whole world before me,
richer because the world as we knew it has stopped.
And I for one am not getting off.

About the Author

Rhonda Liss has enjoyed three diverse careers. She began on the opera, concert, cabaret, and musical theatre stage, singing with the chorus at the Metropolitan Opera, Carnegie Hall, and Radio City Music Hall. She was a soloist at the Netherlands Opera for 14 years, where she played Mrs. Sedley in Peter Grimes. At the Brooklyn Academy of Music, she appeared as Mrs. Alexander in Philip Glass's Satyagraha, which she recorded for CBS. She also performed in London's West End as a soloist, producer, and writer with The Heartache and Sorrow Show and A Canary Called Quintessence, and appeared as Madame Giry in the Toronto company of Phantom of the Opera, directed by Hal Prince. In addition, she has written and performed numerous solo cabarets in New York and Sarasota.

Her second career was as a professor of English as a Second Language at the City University of New York. She is the author of two textbooks for Oxford University Press, including Effective Academic Writing: The Researched Essay.

In her "third act," she is writing, acting, and producing. She has contributed to the production of the Hamptons' Summer Cabaret by the Sea, performed at the Venice Theater in Florida, and appeared in Love Letters in Sarasota. She also writes and performs with the Mark Twain Society, most recently in Fork in the Road: The Dutch Experiment.

Begin I Must is her first book of poetry.

If the mood strikes, send her an email at: rhondaliss@usa.net

Adinkra Symbols Meaning